Bricks & Brickwork in Reading

For much of his 40 years in Reading Adam Sowan has been part of an informal network of people who seek to demonstrate that the town is not just Anywhere: it has its own identity, history, life and culture. This, along with a lifelong interest in words and places, has led him to write a series of books on aspects of the town. He has been for many years an active member of Reading Civic Society.

Other books by Adam Sowan

Believing in Reading: Our places of worship
The Reading Quiz Book
All Change at Reading: The railway and the station 1840–2013
A Much-maligned Town: Opinions of Reading 1126–2008
Abattoirs Road to Zinzan Street: Reading's streets and their names
The Holy Brook or The Granator's Tale: Map and Guide
A Mark of Affection: The Soane Obelisk in Reading
The Stranger in Reading edited by Adam Sowan

Also published by Two Rivers Press

When Reading Really Rocked by Adrian Moulton, Mike Warth & Austin Matthews
Reading's Influential Women by Terry Dixon & Linda Saul
The Art and History of Whiteknights edited by Jenny Halstead
The Art of Peter Hay by John Froy with Martin Andrews
Signs of the Times: Reading's Memorials by Malcolm Summers
Rural Reading by Adrian Lawson & Geoff Sawers
The Constitutionals: A work of fiction by Peter Robinson
Reading Abbey and the Abbey Quarter by Peter Durrant & John Painter
Reading's Bayeux Tapestry by Reading Museum
Picture Palace to Penny Plunge: Reading's Cinemas by David Cliffe
The Shady Side of Town: Reading's Trees by Adrian Lawson & Geoff Sawers
Reading: The Place of the People of the Red One by Duncan Mackay
Silchester: Life on the Dig by Jenny Halstead & Michael Fulford
The Writing on the Wall by Peter Kruschwitz
Caught on Camera: Reading in the 70s by Terry Allsop
Allen W. Seaby: Art and Nature by Martin Andrews & Robert Gillmor
Reading Detectives by Kerry Renshaw
Fox Talbot & the Reading Establishment by Martin Andrews
Caversham Court Gardens: A Heritage Guide by Friends of Caversham Court Gardens
Down by the River: The Thames and Kennet in Reading by Gillian Clark

Bricks & Brickwork in Reading

Patterns & Polychromy

Adam Sowan

First published in the UK in 2020 by Two Rivers Press
7 Denmark Road, Reading RG1 5PA
www.tworiverspress.com

Copyright © Two Rivers Press 2020
Copyright © in text Adam Sowan 2020
Copyright © in 'Decorative brickwork in Reading and the Region: the Victorian Flowering' Jane Wight 1974
Copyright © in photographs resides with the individual photographers. Please refer to picture credits.

The right of Adam Sowan to be identified as the author of the work has been asserted by him in accordance with the Copyright, Designs and Patents Act of 1988.

All rights reserved. No part of this publication may be reproduced, stored in or introduced into a retrieval system, or transmitted, in any form, or by any means (electronic, mechanical, photocopying, recording or otherwise) without the prior written permission of the publisher.

ISBN 978-1-909747-42-5

4 5 6 7 8 9

Two Rivers Press is represented in the UK by Inpress Ltd and distributed by Ingram Publisher Services UK.

Cover photography by Anne Nolan
Cover and text design by Nadja Guggi and typeset in Parisine

Printed and bound in Great Britain by Severn, Gloucester
All materials used in the manufacture of this book are sourced from sustainable forests.

Contents

Preface and acknowledgments | vii
Introduction | 1

I. Bricks | 2

Terminology | 4
How big is a brick? | 5
Colours | 6
An aside on chalk | 9
The story of a brickworks | 12

II. Brickwork | 19

Living back-to-back: how to save bricks and keep warm | 19
On the trail of the crinkle-crankle | 21
A bonding session | 25
Here be dragons | 31
Holey Bricks | 32
It's a cover-up | 33
Alfred Waterhouse: Reading's own architect | 34

Decorative brickwork in Reading and the region:
  The Victorian flowering, by Jane A. Wight | 39

Love your brickwork: Preserve and conserve | 49

III. A walking tour: Town centre & Katesgrove | 53

Preface and acknowledgements

I've been planning this book on Reading's bricks and brickwork for many years. A keen champion of the town, I have explored and appreciated the great variety of brickwork, and pursued research into various aspects relating to the use and production of bricks. As a diligent defender of the unnoticed and undervalued, I'm particularly interested in brick features such as crinkle crankle walls, Reading's own back-to-backs, holey bricks and terracotta dragons. As well as my own work, I very much wanted to include Jane Wight's research on the town's decorative brickwork, and information culled from Don Macgregor's work on S & E Collier Ltd, the brick makers. I would like to thank the Two Rivers Press team for their help in completing this tribute to one of Reading's most prominent features – the humble brick.

Adam Sowan, October 2020

Acknowledgements

Photographer Anne Nolan accompanied me on long walks around Reading while I instructed her where to point her camera. Managing Publisher Sally Mortimore has tackled my copious notes, wrestling with my terrible handwriting, done some more research, and with the help of editor Anke Ueberberg produced sections on the bricks and brickworks. Picture research and photography has been carried out by various members of the team, whose attempts to capture Reading's brickwork have been made beautiful by Nadja Guggi's digital skills. I'd also like to thank Jane Wight for permission to reproduce her article, 'Decorative brickwork in Reading and Region: the Victorian Flowering'. And Barbara Norburn, her niece, for corresponding with me. Finally, I'd like to acknowledge Don Macgregor's biographical work on S & E Collier Ltd, a bound copy of which can be found in Reading Library.

Publisher's acknowledgements

Two Rivers Press would like to thank RG Spaces for their generous grant towards this book which has made it possible to reproduce the photographs in colour. And we would like to acknowledge the support of our community which has enabled us to keep publishing despite the disruption to our business that COVID-19 caused, and to thank the following for their sponsorship of this publication: Alison Bennett, Jane Club (UK) and Anke Ueberberg.

Picture credits

© James Birtwistle: viii, 7

© Terry Allsop: 15

© Reading Museum (Reading Borough Council). All rights reserved: 11

© John Meredith/Online Transport Archive: 17

Anne Nolan: 1, 3, 6, 13–14, 18, 22–24, 29–32, 37, 41–42, 44–46, 48–50, 51 (Wokingham Road), 54, 55 (Chancellors), 56–57, 58 (Flemish Garden Wall), 59–60, 61 (Castle Tap, Castle Street), 62–63

Nadja Guggi: 25, 27 (Christchurch Road), 28, 35–36, 39–41, 43, 50 (Field Road), 52–53

Sally Mortimore: 6, 8, 15 (Samuel J. Collier's grave), 27 (Palmer Building), 33, 51 (School Terrace), 55 (Market House), 58 (Church Street), 61 (Cross Keys)

The Kennet & Avon Canal depicted in brickwork at Kenavon Drive (demolished in 2019)

Opposite page:
Decorative brickwork on Christchurch Road

Introduction

The '3 Bs' of Reading, as anyone will tell you, were beer, bulbs and biscuits, the products that made Reading prosper in the 19th and 20th centuries. Dominated at the time by Simonds Brewery, Sutton Seeds and Huntley & Palmers, these industries have all gone, but they were not the only ones for which the town was well known. Reading had printing, food stuffs (sauces and jams), cloth and light and heavy engineering, including a few more Bs: boat building, metal boxes (for the biscuits) and bricks: the prime candidate for the fourth B. Not only were bricks *made* here – Reading was, until not so long ago, almost entirely built of them.

The only local building stone was flint, still to be seen in the oldest buildings and in the Abbey ruins, where the cores of the walls were made from flint and the soft chalk that Reading is built on. The Abbey's walls were originally encased in honey-coloured limestone from Taynton, near Burford in Oxfordshire. There was also a brief enthusiasm for Bath stone, which was transported to Reading on the Kennet & Avon Canal from 1810 and on the Great Western Railway in the 1830s and 40s. Brick came back into fashion in Victorian times and was used for buildings great – the Town Hall for example – and small. Although the Gothic fashion for decorative detail was a bit passé, brickmakers in Reading went for it: patterns and polychromy proliferated, fashioned by builders of even the humblest houses in back streets and terraces.

It is the latter, with their obscure but inventive colours and patterns, that are most striking to the author, and to many visitors to Reading.

What follows is neither a treatise on brick nor a technical account of brickmaking, or a list of local buildings: it's a tribute to a town made unique by its builders, and a bid to inspire you to see the beauty of its brickwork yourself.

Opposite page:
Mary Lyne Almshouses,
New Lane Hill, Tilehurst

I. Bricks

As building technologies go, bricks are among the very oldest. Fired bricks made of red clay were used as flooring in Neolithic China around 4400 BC, and kilns were widely used in Britain since Roman times. In Reading, a medieval tile kiln was discovered in Silver Street in 2001, and the name 'Tilehurst' comes from Old English and means 'a wooded hill where tiles are made'. The Tudors used brick for such architectural feats as Hampton Court and St James's Palace, but it really took off as the building material of choice during the house-building boom in the years leading up to World War I.

Various factors came together to create the perfect context for Reading to be a brick-built town: the quality of the clay beds, especially around the Kennet; the unique red colour of the fired bricks, owing to the local clay's high iron content; the availability and accessibility of chalk; and the explosion of the population in Victorian times, caused by the migration from countryside to town in the wake of the rise of industry and the railway.

The 1860 *Mineral Statistics of the United Kingdom of Great Britain and Ireland* (also known as Hunts Mineral Statistics) contains a list of brickworks and brick kilns operating in 1858, along with their owners. Of 35 brick and tile works in Berkshire, about 11 were in or around Reading, including Castle Kiln and Coley Kiln owned by Samuel Collier; Caversham Kiln (or Brickfield), Waterloo Kiln (Caversham) and Waterloo Kiln (Reading) owned by John Leach; Erleigh Court Kiln (or Brickfield); Katesgrove Kiln owned by E. Salter & Co; and Rose Kiln owned by Philbrick.

The distinction between a brickfield and a kiln in the report may have signified sites without permanent kilns that burned bricks in 'clamps'. The Waterloos were presumably named to commemorate the defeat of Napoleon on 18 June 1815, so perhaps commenced operation at that time. The Rose Kiln name lives on in a modern road.

Terminology

Given the loss of many brick-making terms from our language, some terminology will help to set the scene.

Brick-clay has a high clay content and is suited to pottery and tile making due to its elasticity. **Brick-earth**, on the other hand, has a much lower clay content and is suited to making standard bricks. Brick manufacturing didn't require a major capital outlay aside from ownership of the relevant piece of land rich in brick-earth. The topsoil was simply removed to expose the clay layer, which was easily dug, moulded and kilned, often all on one site.

A **tingle plate** is a small piece of metal sandwiched between two bricks (the lower of which is called the tingle brick) in the middle of the mason's line to stop it sagging.

A **chariot recessed jointing tool** is vital for producing an even finish when recessed jointing has been employed: the heavy shadow lines that such jointing creates show up any defects in bricks or brickwork so it's important to ensure the mortar face is even and unbroken.

Weep holes are small openings left between bricks, often near the bottom of retaining walls, to allow water to escape.

Spalling is when bricks crack or splinter and bits flake off, often due to freeze-thawing if water is trapped inside.

Queen closers are required to maintain the regularity of pattern in some types of bond, such as Flemish and English Garden Wall bonds. The Queen closer is a brick cut in half lengthways, whereas a **half bat** is one that is cut in half across the width.

Putlog holes are openings left in walls to slot beams or poles (putlogs) into to build or support scaffolding.

How big is a brick?

The autumn 2015 bulletin of Insight (published by Farmer & Dyer) tells us that Robert Plot, an English naturalist, first professor of Chemistry at the University of Oxford, and the first keeper of the Ashmolean Museum, noted brickmaking in this locality in 1705, observing that 'they make a sort of brick 22 inches long and above 6 inches broad'. The dimensions of bricks have changed very little over the years, but 19th-century or 'Imperial' bricks were larger than both their Elizabethan predecessors and modern ones.

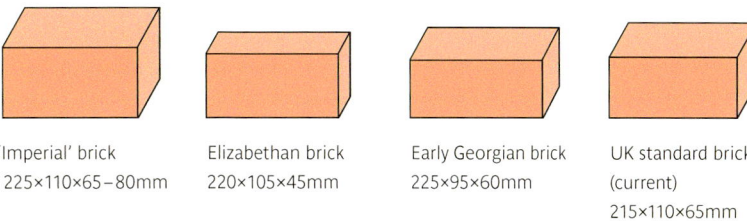

'Imperial' brick
225×110×65–80mm

Elizabethan brick
220×105×45mm

Early Georgian brick
225×95×60mm

UK standard brick
(current)
215×110×65mm

The measurements above are approximate as bricks vary considerably in size, depending on where in the country and by whom they're made, and the shrinkage during firing.

In the late 18th century, the size of bricks was also influenced by taxation. The brick tax was introduced in 1784 to help pay for the war in America; manufacturers were charged 2s 6d per thousand bricks. In response, they increased the size of their bricks. The government then limited the dimensions to 10×5×3in (or 150 cubic inches) and doubled the tax on larger bricks (10 inches is 254mm). The tax was finally abolished in 1850.

Newtown Primary School

Yellow and grey bricks laid in a diamond pattern, Pell Street/Sherman Road junction

Opposite page: Decorated gable at Reading School

Colours

Reading's brick is praised in brick fancier circles for its strong red colour, but J.E. Vincent, describing Reading's manufacturing heart in *The Story of the Thames*, 1909, was less enthusiastic. He bemoaned the 'endless streets of plain and staring red-brick houses' and advised the visitor that it is 'not wise to land at Reading in search of objects of interest – they are few and far between'.

The colour of a town's bricks is dictated by the type of clay it rests upon. In Cambridgeshire it's almost yellow; in Oxfordshire it's beige. Impurities in the clay such as iron oxide and the 'recipe' the brickmaker used (varying quantities of added sand, chalk, ash, and even the amount of smoke in the kiln) as well as the firing temperature all create variations. Mixing

Silver-grey frontages give way to red sides on Alexandra Road

chalk with the brick-earth makes the colour of the resulting bricks lighter, improves the quality of the final brick and prevents shrinkage during firing.

In Reading, chalk can be found not far below the surface; John Poulton, who founded the Waterloo Kiln at Katesgrove, produced Reading's silver-grey bricks – perhaps those that grace the frontages of larger houses along London Road, Alexandra Road and Elmhurst Road. These bricks were more expensive than the humbler red ones, and you'll notice that they tend to give way to red on the sides and backs of the houses.

An aside on chalk

Reading's reliance on bricks meant the manufacturers needed a ready supply of chalk; fortunately, there is plenty of it under our streets. One interesting chalk mine is in Emmer Green: Hanover Mine, now closed off but accessible occasionally. Paul Sowan, the author's brother, was given access to it on 25 January 2004.

He was intrigued by graffiti found incised in a joint plane close to the shaft and pencilled on the wall near the borehole. It seems that a number of people, presumably visitors to the mine rather than workers, left their mark on the walls. Family or local historians may recognise some of the names:

1857 W Hunt, The Grove, Caversham
1879 W C
1886 J East
1889 (17 November) William Taylor Mal-?
1889 (19 November) John Cox, Sonning Common
1892 Seymour East
1894 (May) E J Ward
1894 B Ruddock
1897 (11 May) N S Ive
1908 (25 March) W Townsend
1908 G Bullen
1908 J Dance
1941 (3 December) C Loram RCED?
1941 S May
1941 W E C McIlroy (who tells us he was the mayor)
1942 (10 February) P C Green
Undated:
W Seymour
Chase E Fidler
James Jeffery

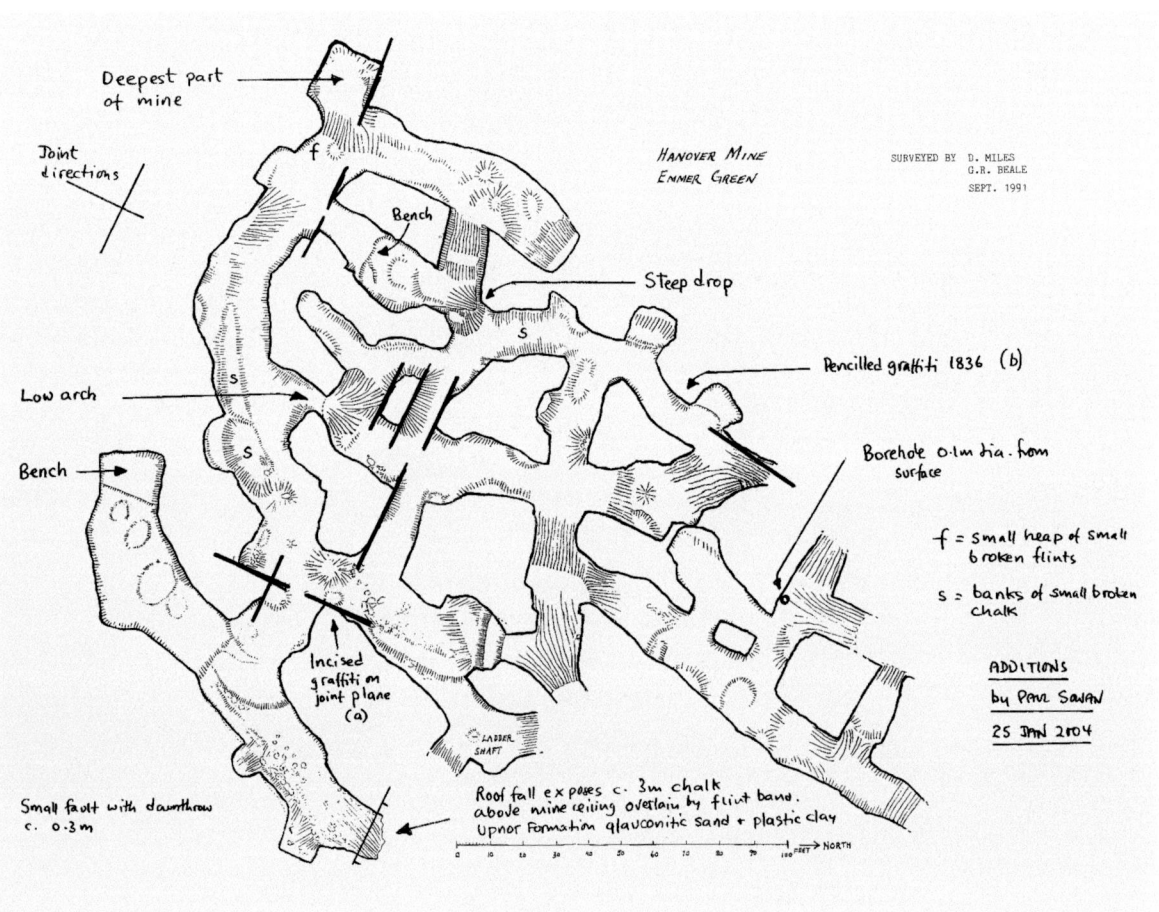

Field Road in Coley is one of several areas in Reading that have suffered from subsidence damage since the 1950s

Opposite page:
Map of Hanover Mine, Emmer Green, annotated by Paul Sowan 25 January 2004

Technically, Hanover Mine consisted of two mines joined together – possibly accidentally – each with its own *c*.70ft shaft. During World War II, Reading Council stored its archives and valuables there, moving loose chalk about to create a roadway (and leaving behind their bottles of ink). Polish tins with holes in their lids and filled with silica gel kept the papers dry.

The chalk mine in Field Road, off Castle Hill, is infamous. When it was closed in 1830, there was no law requiring its registration. In January 2000, the mine, long forgotten, caved in: two houses and the road surface partly collapsed, thirty houses had to be evacuated, and it took up to two years before residents could return to their homes. Further investigations in 2005 and 2011 were followed by more stabilisation measures. But even before these events, the collapse of the new swimming pool at Coley Primary School in Wolseley Street in 1994 – just a few days before it was due to open – may have been caused by abandoned mines: the pool was situated at the base of the hill that led to Field Road. Several cave-ins in Palmer Park in 2001 remained unexplained but the holes were filled in and the ground stabilised sufficiently to allow funfairs to operate in the park again.

Opposite page:
Pell Street – a Collier showcase

The story of a brickworks

Don McGregor's unpublished biographical research notes, 'S & E Collier Ltd and Silchester Ware Pottery', provide a detailed company history of S & E Collier and give a good picture of the brick industry in Reading in the 19th century. This section is substantially based on his notes.

S & E Collier was one of the town's most prolific, successful and long-lasting 'tilemakers and brickmakers', operating for more than 100 years before closure in 1967. Whole streets in West Reading showcase Collier bricks and tiles.

Hunt's 1860 list of brickworks contains two entries relating to Samuel Collier, the founder, who moved to Reading from Witney around 1830, apprenticed as a Tallow-Chandler. In 1840, he is listed as a glass and china dealer operating in Broad Street, and in 1848 he took the lease on Coley Hill Kiln, presumably to provide his successful sales business with a manufacturing arm.

Many small brick and tile works also created terracotta items for architectural purposes (chimney pots) and home use (plant pots – red ware, and household pottery – brown ware). When Samuel's sons, Samuel Jeremiah and Edward Philip, joined the business, they operated several different kiln sites in the Coley area. The Hunt entries from 1860 are:

Kiln	Castle Kiln, Reading
Formation	Reading Beds (Plastic Clay)
Freeholder	J Bushell Esq
Manufacturer	Samuel Collier
Output p.a.	bricks 750,000; socket pipes 20,000; best red ware 5,000.

Kiln	Coley Kiln, Reading
Formation	Reading Beds (Plastic Clay)
Freeholder	–
Manufacturer	Samuel Collier
Output p.a.	red bricks (see Katesgrove)

Queen Victoria Street

Opposite page:
King's Road Baptist church, built in 1834 and photographed by Terry Allsop in the 1970s

Samuel Jeremiah's grave in Old Reading Cemetery, London Road

Samuel Collier died at his home on Coley Avenue in 1865 aged 53, 'a Town Councillor for 17 years and a Poor Law Guardian' (from the *Reading Mercury* 2 December 1865). The two brothers – the S and E of S&E Collier – continued to run the business, moving to Grovelands, Tilehurst, in 1877, when the clay supply available at Coley was used up. Samuel Jeremiah's oldest son of 11 children, Samuel George, entered the business and was made a partner in around 1887. Samuel Jeremiah's second son, William Edward, also worked in the business but left *c.*1888 to found, with James Catley, the building business Collier & Catley, which became a major house builder in Reading. Today it is a specialist builder whose recent projects include the Falklands War memorial chapel at Pangbourne College and the Oakwood Centre in Woodley.

Samuel Jeremiah Collier died in 1890. The funeral took place at the King's Road Baptist Church, where the family were active members, and he is buried in Old Reading Cemetery, London Road.

The Grovelands Works was well established by the 1890s, with four factories making pottery, tiles and bricks. Terracotta from the works graces Queen Victoria Street, the Art Gallery extension of the Town Hall and Grovelands Baptist Church. An article in the April 1895 edition of *The British Clayworker* includes a report of S & E Collier's stand at the Building Trades Exhibition and praises the specialities of Grovelands clay – 'its exceedingly bright red colour… if anything, brighter in body than on the surface' and its fine texture.

By 1902 S & E Collier had become a limited company, and the Grovelands works were described in a report in the *Reading Standard* (8 November 1902) as

> five factories, one large clay pit within the works but the bulk of the clay is obtained from a pit in Prospect Park (on lease from Corporation of Reading) and brought to the Works by an overhead wire rope railway of about ⅛ mile. Output of the firm is 25–30,000 tons of red clay goods per annum, 250–300 hands employed.

A non-conformist with a family history of civic duty and charity involvement, Edward Collier objected to parts of the 1902 Education Act, which required the teaching of religious principles and creeds that he thought erroneous. The family became part of a national Passive Resistance Movement and deducted sums that they thought would be applied to the rate-supported voluntary schools from their Borough Rate payments. When Reading Borough Council sued for the outstanding debts, 110 people appeared in court. Warrants were issued that led to the seizure and auction of personal goods to satisfy the debts. Rate demands issued every six months, court appearances and the seizure and sale of goods became a recurrent and good-natured event between 1903 and 1905; at an auction in 1904 Edward Collier bought back two office chairs,

Opposite page:
Norcot Road under the aerial ropeway of S. E. Collier's Brick & Tile Works, Grovelands, 1 July 1951

company property that had already been sold four times for the same purpose! When Edward died in 1919 aged 71, the obituaries praised his devotion to the Baptist cause and his public service, particularly in education: he had become a member of the School Board in *c.*1888, been elected to the Council and been Chairman of the Education Committee for 15 years.

In 1904 the company terminated the lease in Prospect Park because the clay had been worked out, and in August 1905 they acquired the brick and tile-making business of Messrs Poulton & Son at Waterloo Kiln. The Kennet clay beds near Waterloo Road and Elgar Road were praised for their size, depth and quality.

In 1907 an ancient cooking pit containing a number of medieval pottery vessels was discovered at Waterloo Kiln. There is some evidence to suggest the kiln was in existence as far back as 1770. A number of Roman remains had also been found in the vicinity, suggesting that a settlement existed there during the Roman occupation. All these finds were donated by Colliers to Reading Museum and were believed to be Roman but later identified as Norman/medieval by the curator. They aren't currently on display, although several fossils from Waterloo Pit are.

By 1924 Colliers were looking for additional clay land. They bought just over four acres from J. Martin and William P. Routh which were connected to existing Collier-owned land via two aerial ropeways, and in 1925 they purchased 36 acres of land at Hilltop, adjacent to Tilehurst Potteries. A brand-new aerial ropeway was built which brought the total to three. Ropeways 1 & 2 from the clay pit to a transfer station and then on across Water Road, with Ropeway 3 to carry clay, sand etc. from Hilltop to the Groveland Works. Completed in 1926, the new ropeways, the new clay pit at Hilltop and increased power plant capacity at Grovelands led to the highest-ever gross profit being recorded in 1928. The company provided facing bricks for the Shakespeare Memorial Theatre in Stratford.

During the early war years production was greatly reduced. Buildings at Grovelands and Waterloo were requisitioned by the Government for

storage, and land at Hilltop for military training. In 1951 Waterloo Kiln was sold and converted into a foundry, and in 1960 the aerial ropeway used to convey buckets of clay from Hilltop to Grovelands was demolished. In April 1967 Groveland Works closed; now it's occupied by the Water Road estate. In 1969, the Dee Road estate was built partly on the site of the Collier clay pit. A memorial honouring employees of S & E Collier Ltd killed in the World Wars stands at the side of Water Road.

Opposite page:
A variety of brick colours, tones and shades graces Blake's Lock, Gas Works Road

II. Brickwork

Bricks and terracotta can be structural or decorative, and Reading has a wealth of brickwork which is both. A rich variety of bonds, patterns, polychromy and decorative terracotta can be found all over town.

Living back-to-back: how to save bricks and keep warm

A rectangular detached house has four outside walls; a semi has three; a terraced two. But around the corner from Birmingham New Street station the National Trust has preserved some one-wall houses known as 'back-to-backs', with no rear windows or gardens. Some had three rooms, one above the other. They were common in the North and the Midlands, notably in Leeds and Nottingham, but very rare south of a line from Bristol to Ipswich, and Reading's little-known set were a one-off.

The area around Chatham Street was once part of Battle Farm, which had belonged to Battle Abbey, near Hastings. Development for housing started in 1817, in the form of a nearly symmetrical grid of wide, terraced streets: Chatham, Weldale, Great Knollys and Bedford. Between them were the narrower Caroline, William and Charles streets, with smaller houses. However, a long, narrow part of the site between Chatham and Weldale Street had been dug out for a gravel pit and, at the same time, was developed for housing in the form of 56 back-to-backs: the rear walls of Somerset Place were also the rear walls of Warren Place.

The Pit, as the area came to be known, was a seriously unhealthy place, with no surface drains, only four privies, two water taps which only worked for twelve hours every other day, and two cesspools. A man who was trying to empty one of them was suffocated by noxious vapours.

The local press reported regular outbreaks of crime and violence committed by residents of both sexes. There were domestic rows, wife-beating, assaults (victims included policemen and 'an old deformed man'), affrays; firing of a gun in a public street, being drunk and disorderly or riotous;

trespass, breach of the peace by making 'rough music' – beating a frying pan with a stick; indecent exposure; and serving out of hours at the beer-house. Theft, including highway robbery and poaching, was commonplace. Purloined items included money (a prostitute stole a guinea, probably from a client); a spoon; mutton and suet; but also (even more) low-value loot that indicates the depth of poverty in the area: pieces of carpet, flowers and roots, even swede tops. Two pig-dealers fought over a handful of hay.

The local papers enjoyed reporting the sordid details of life in the Pit: one article referred to

> a locality the inhabitants thereof are wont to relieve the monotony of existence by a little neighbourly squabbling amongst themselves. Their little domestic dramas are all pretty much alike... The complainant and defendant live in that healthful and charming locality... the case arose from one of those disgraceful fights which recur from time to time amongst the very pugnacious inhabitants...

In 1922 the back-to-backs were demolished, and the Thames Valley Traction Co built a bus garage on the site. In 1967 this was swept away in favour of an unbeautiful multi-storey car park with a few shops. These have now given way to Chatham Place.

On the trail of the crinkle-crankle

Almost all garden walls are straight, unless they follow an undulating or irregular boundary; and retaining walls on sloping ground may consist of a series of concave curves, with or without piers, for strength. Crinkle-crankle (or wavy or serpentine) walls, however, could have been straight but are deliberately not. The most satisfying and purest form of crinkle is a simple, regular in-and-out wave, but the term also includes a repeating series of curves all facing the same way. It is generally accepted that there are both aesthetic and practical reasons for crinkling.

First, they are pleasing to the eye, making a softer boundary and creating patterns and gradations of light and shade. Second, their hollows or angles are said to provide a little extra shelter from the wind and reflect direct heat (and return retained heat) onto delicate plants or trees. Third, the curves and angles undoubtedly have a self-buttressing effect. They can therefore be thinner and, in theory, cheaper to build than a straight wall; but it is likely that a bricklayer would charge more for the additional skill and time required, outweighing any savings on materials.

The great age of crinkling, from *c.*1780 to *c.*1820, roughly corresponded to the era of folly-building and playful, pre-Pugin Gothic (or Gothick) architecture. Crinkling more or less died out by 1850 and is absent from many areas, suggesting that the claimed advantages were not significant: it was largely a fad, albeit an endearing one. There are (or were) well over 200 examples in England; the typical habitat is a manor house or rectory, often enclosing the kitchen garden. The distribution is weighted heavily towards East Anglia, perhaps suggesting Dutch origin; they thin out to the west and north. There is a marked tendency to cluster, suggesting that friends and family of crinkle-owners visited and said 'I want one of those'. Clumps can be found along the Hampshire coast and around Guildford in Surrey, and crinkles are or were to be found in Englefield, Pangbourne, Shinfield and Theale. Reading ensures that Berkshire comes fourth in the county league tables. The local set is uncharacteristically late in date and urban in setting.

Above: Crinkle-crankle and remains of a heated wall with flues in the buttresses, Caversham Court Gardens

Opposite page: Crinkle-crankle, Caversham Court Gardens

Church Road, Caversham: Caversham Court

A 4m high, 80m long retaining wall remains between the church above and allotments – formerly the garden of the Old Rectory – below. Cusped with piers and primarily built for strength, it has 12 irregular bays with some short straights and uses the Flemish Garden Wall bond. 'A.E. 1774' is scratched into the brickwork. Restoration work in 2009 revealed traces of whitewash, suggesting that at some time there may have been a lean-to glasshouse. In the same garden is the remains of a heated wall with flues in the buttresses, *c*.1820, heightened *c*.1880.

Crinkle-crankle, Bath Road, north side, between Lima Court and the Spire Dunedin Hospital

Opposite page:
'Dull and repetitive' Stretcher bond brought to life in multi-colour, Elmhurst Road

A tightly-curved section calling for Header bond, Yield Hall Place

Bath Road, north side, between Lima Court and the Spire Dunedin Hospital (see 'A walking tour')

This short, low remaining fragment of a 180ft wall of 11 15ft bays is the only publicly visible example apart from Caversham Court. It is the last survivor of a set of seven crinkles, most of them on the south side of the road, around large detached villas dating from the 1840s. Four of them had crinkles on both sides and to the rear. The party walls were 300ft, with 18 15ft bays, and the rear wall 400ft long.

Francis Street and Pell Street (see 'A walking tour')

This 8-bay wall now separates the back gardens of the two streets, and its waviness serves no structural or decorative purpose; but an 1853 map shows it as a free-standing wall inside the premises of the Katesgrove brickworks. It would therefore seem to have been either an apprentice piece or an advertisement, demonstrating a variety of colours, bonds or quality, and as such may be a unique survival.

Coley Hill
Two party walls behind houses on the east side.

Mapledene, off Chazey Road, Caversham
A wavy ha-ha, *c*.1990, in a front garden.

Oxford Road and Zinzan Street
Five 100ft party walls to terraced houses near the corner, *c*.1850. 20ft wavelength. Two may survive.

Friar Street
South side, behind no. 73: two 20ft bays. On 1853 map: demolished.

London Road
No. 41, now part of Kendrick School had three internal garden walls, *c*.500ft in total, behind a house of *c*.1800. All demolished.

Whitley Street, west side, near the south end
A single party wall between small terraced houses, *c*.1850, demolished.

A bonding session

A bond is the way bricks are arranged to make a wall. A standard brick has six faces, two each of three dimensions: a statute of 1571 ruled that they should measure 9×4.5×2.25in, a size that one large hand can hold. Normally the largest face looks up or down and is not seen (but see Rat-trap bond below). The long, narrow side is called a stretcher, and the smallest is the header. The bonds most commonly used are:

Header: and nothing but, with all bricks visible. This makes it expensive, because they all have to be respectable 'facing' bricks, with no cheap 'common' ones. This bond thus demonstrates some wealth. The Georgian houses on London Street and Castle Street show many examples, often in silver-grey. Header bond is also found in sharply curved walls to avoid protruding angles.

Stretcher: and nothing but. Brick-fanciers dismiss this bond as dull and repetitive. Almost universally used since c.1900, it nearly always denotes a cavity wall.

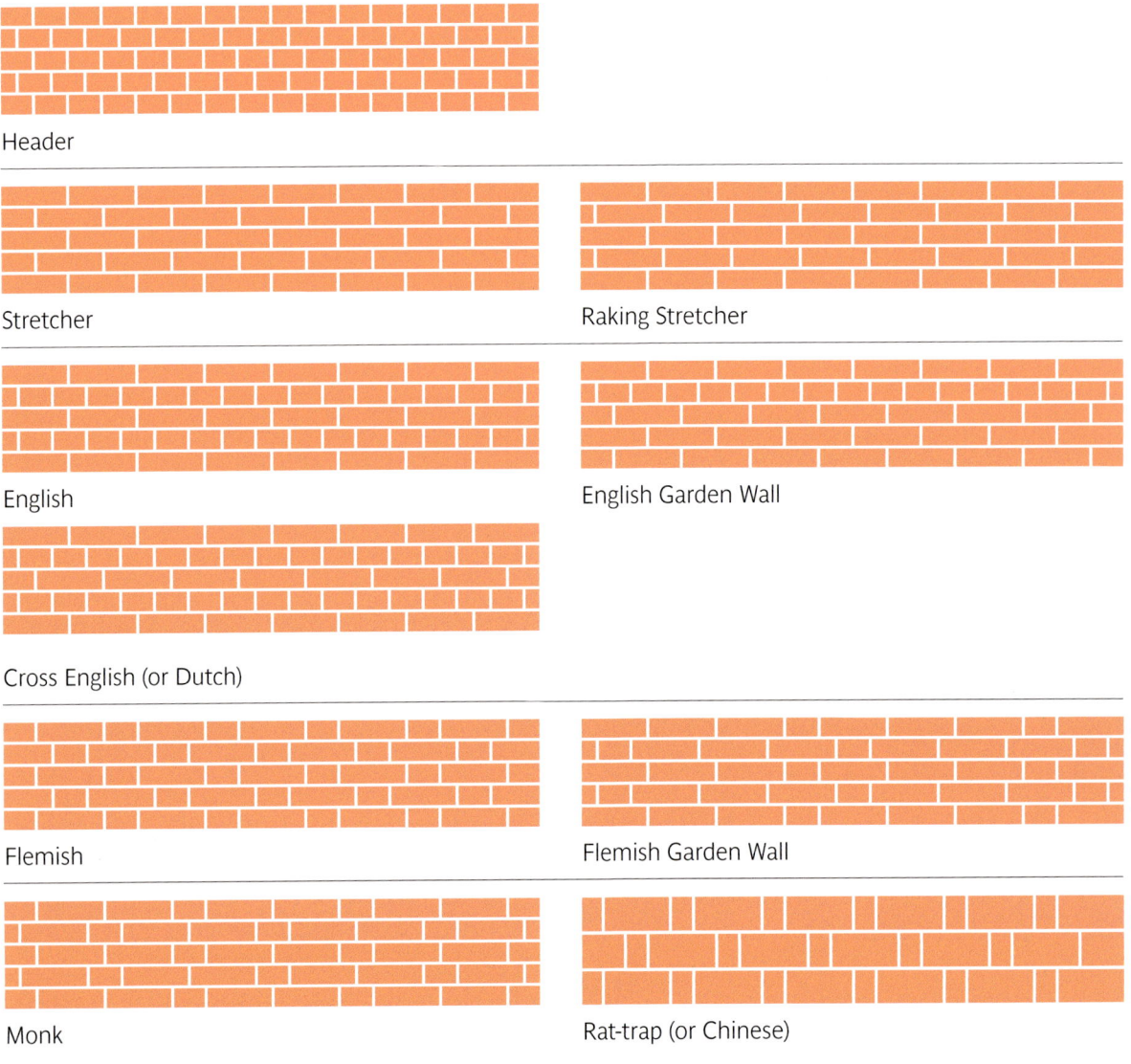

Common types of brick bond

Header

Stretcher

Raking Stretcher

English

English Garden Wall

Cross English (or Dutch)

Flemish

Flemish Garden Wall

Monk

Rat-trap (or Chinese)

Raking Stretcher bond, Palmer Building, University of Reading Whiteknights campus

English bond was used for large, prestigious buildings such as this, 39 Christchurch Road

Raking Stretcher: a rare and welcome variant in which the bricks are offset by a third or a quarter of a brick instead of the usual half.

English: the first proper bond to emerge out of medieval irregularity. Courses (layers) of all-headers and all-stretchers alternate pleasingly. Used everywhere before *c*.1650, it is reckoned the strongest bond because it has the fewest through joints. It was largely supplanted by Flemish, but continued to be used for large, prestigious or industrial buildings.

Cross English or **Dutch:** a variant in which the stretchers are not vertically aligned, giving a very busy look. It's almost unknown in England but the norm all over the Low Countries.

Flemish bond, Elgar Road

Flemish: each course has alternating headers and stretchers, giving a pleasing balance. First used at Kew Palace in 1631, it reigned throughout the land from c.1650 to c.1900. The name is a puzzle: extensive travels in Flanders have found only a handful of examples in such bricky cities as Ghent. Britannica confusingly says Flemish is also called Dutch; and the first use in the Oxford English dictionary is a quote from 1777: 'the Flemish Bond is the strongest as well as the oldest regular bond used in building'. This sounds like English bond, and our current usage perhaps arose from an ambiguously worded traveller's description. The Germans call it Polish Bond.

Both of these last two common bonds have cheaper variants:
English Garden Wall has three or five stretcher courses between the headers, and in **Flemish Garden Wall** each course has three or five stretchers between each pair of headers. These bonds are not confined to the garden, and are safe for two-storey houses.

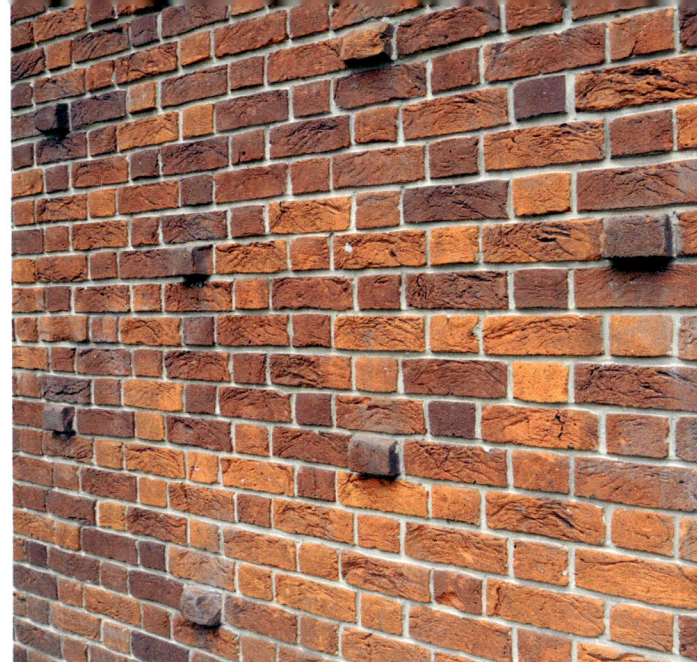

A unique example of Rat trap bond using overburned bricks, Wokingham Road

Burglar bond, Düsseldorf Way

Monk: uses two stretchers and a header repeating, giving an unrestful, jerky effect. There is a rather unintentional-looking patch on the side of a dentist's on Bridge Street, Caversham; Guildford Cathedral, begun in 1937 and never a monastery, shows a vast vertical acreage of Monk.

Rat-trap or Chinese: the idea of laying bricks precariously on their narrow sides should perhaps be anathema to a professional brickie, but most examples are an early and reasonably strong version of a cavity wall (with plenty of room for rats). Found in numerous garden walls in Eastern Avenue and surrounding streets, and occasionally in houses.

Burglar: an unofficial name for any bond having projecting bricks, regularly or randomly: helpful for thieves with some skill in rock-climbing.

Other, sometimes nameless bonds occur: try the University's clocktower, or the side of the Pavilion church on the Oxford Road (formerly the Gaumont cinema) or Elizabeth House in Gosbrook Road – which last might be labelled Raking English Garden Wall.

The old Hillingdon Prince Hotel, 39 Christchurch Road

Opposite page:
The Griffin, Church Road, Caversham

Here be dragons

Most Reading houses are squarish brick boxes with pitched roofs of good Welsh slate. Where two slopes meet, they form a ridge; you can't bend slate, so along the top of the ridge we find tiles in the form of an inverted 'V'. Unadorned, these can look very plain, so they are often fretted or pierced to enliven the skyline. At the ridge-ends there is frequently a decorative finial, most commonly of a stylised vegetal design, but occasionally they are fierce terracotta dragons, reminiscent of Norwegian stave churches. Examples can be seen near Honey End Lane, on the Griffin pub in Church Road, Caversham, and the old hotel opposite Henley station.

Air brick at the Town Hall

Opposite page:
Air bricks at Wycliffe Baptist Church, King's Road

Holey Bricks

Buildings that have suspended wooden floors over a void need ventilation to prevent damp. This is achieved by replacing one or more ordinary bricks at ground level with 'air bricks', which are pierced with holes too small for the tiniest rodent to squeeze through. The holes can be arranged in a simple grid or form mildly decorative patterns. More recently, clay air bricks have been largely superseded by metal plates or louvres, but millions of bricks survive, hardly noticed in the street scene.

Larger and more prestigious edifices make a virtue of necessity, with elaborate designs placed conspicuously. The Town Hall boasts a fine set of air bricks round the curve at the Art Gallery end: within a large rectangular brick is a swirly design that, in architectural terms, might be called curvilinear gothic. A plainer, but still conspicuous, version can be seen along the west flank of Wycliffe church in King's Road, with two outliers on a house in Denmark Road: one suspects that they were surplus to the church's needs and 'borrowed' by the builder.

It's a cover-up

Reading, like many towns, has more brickwork than meets the eye. When stone was fashionable but expensive, particularly in Regency times, builders would use cheap bricks and encase them in plaster or stucco, which could be made to resemble stonework by incising fake joints. Later, in the 1920s and 30s, undisguised plaster, harl, pebbledash or roughcast likewise hid common brickwork. Other forms of outer skin were hung tiles or slates; the latter were especially popular along the South Coast, giving protection against the wet and salty westerly winds. Later still, homeowners started to personalise their houses in various ways – notably replacing wooden sashes with UPVC casement windows and covering up perfectly good brickwork with paint or stone cladding.

In a sort of reverse movement, in late Georgian times someone thought of a wheeze to avoid the Brick Tax: tiles that looked like bricks. Known as 'mathematical' tiles, alluding to the precise engineering required to produce them, they were popular along the Sussex coast, particularly in Brighton and Lewes. None have been noted in Reading, but there are two lots in Hungerford High Street that exemplify two ways in which one can detect mathematicals: sometimes, odd tiles in a 'course', will slip downwards as full bricks wouldn't; and when a wall reaches a corner or window, you may see the tiles end-on.

Foxhill House, University of Reading, Whiteknights campus

Alfred Waterhouse: Reading's own architect

Anyone with an interest in Reading's built heritage will find Sidney Gold's *Biographical Dictionary of Architects at Reading* an indispensable work of reference. Its pages show that most buildings in and around town whose designer is known were the work of a limited number of strictly local practices. Some were very talented – the Billings and Briants in the early 19th century, and later Joseph Morris and his family and associates. Others – competent, versatile and prolific – included the Smiths, Frederick Albury, and the Ravenscrofts. But the roll-call also includes a dozen-and-a-half men known nationally: mainstream Victorians like Blomfield, Bodley, Butterfield and Street, as well as later individualists such as Ninian Comper, Frank Matcham, Richard Norman Shaw and Clough Williams-Ellis. Alas, their contributions to the local scene often amounted to no more than a chancel here, an aisle there; a war memorial, a pair of gates, or unspecified alterations to older buildings; and much of their work has been demolished.

Four particularly famous names do, however, stand out: John Soane, whose Simonds brewery and brewer's house were lost in 1900 but who retains a prominent presence in the Simeon obelisk in the Market Place; A.W. Pugin, high priest of the Gothic Revival, who built St James's RC church in a neo-Norman style; George Gilbert Scott, who designed Reading Gaol in an early partnership with William Moffat; and, of course, Alfred Waterhouse, who lived in the town for ten years before moving out to Yattendon. Reading has three of his major works – the southern end of the Town Hall, Reading School, and his own house at Foxhill – and a number of other houses, churches and educational buildings. This legacy, and his evident delight in the local bricks and terracotta, make Waterhouse very much Reading's own architect. He is known for vast and important projects such as Manchester Town Hall, the Natural History Museum in South Kensington and the fiery-red Prudential headquarters in Holborn (which earned him the nickname 'Slaughterhouse Waterhouse'). His jobs

Reading Town Hall

in and around Reading total some 36 commissions and attributions. Twenty-eight are within the current Borough boundary or the University campus; 13 of these survive as more or less whole buildings. Here is a list of the more important ones, which are all brick.

1865–6: Caversham Free Church, Gosbrook Road, later the West Memorial Institute, now converted to flats and named 'Waterhouse'.

1867: Foxhill, Whiteknights, his own house, now the University's School of Law.

1868–72: Reading School, Erleigh Road, a classic Waterhouse skyline, but more symmetrical than it first appears. The main hall was designed to accommodate all 100 boys.

1874–6: Reading School Chapel.

1870–7: Christchurch Parsonage, Vicarage Road, now the Early Years Centre of the Abbey Junior School; a dark and rather haunted-looking place.

1874–6: Municipal Buildings (Reading Town Hall) (see 'A walking tour'). *Murray's Berkshire Architectural Guide* (Betjeman & Piper, 1949) dismisses the work of Waterhouse and Lainson here as 'not beautiful'. In 1960 Cedric Pulford wrote 'Reading Town Hall is an acquired taste', and of the later parts he says,

> no effort appears to have been made to match the bricks, which is a pity, for the extension, with its greyer greys and redder reds, is decidedly sombre. The whole composition is very free Gothic. There are lapses, but as representative architecture the buildings are not without interest.

The second edition of Pevsner describes the light grey bricks with red brick trim as 'an unusually soft palette for Waterhouse'.

1875–77: Somerleaze, 30 Christchurch Road, with stables and cottages, now the Abbey Junior School. The grey and yellow bricks might put the Waterhouse-hunter off the scent; truncated chimneys spoil the skyline.

1876–77: Caversham Baptist Church, corner of Gosbrook Road/Prospect Street.

1877: Rising Sun Coffee House, 30 Silver Street, now the Rising Sun Arts Centre.

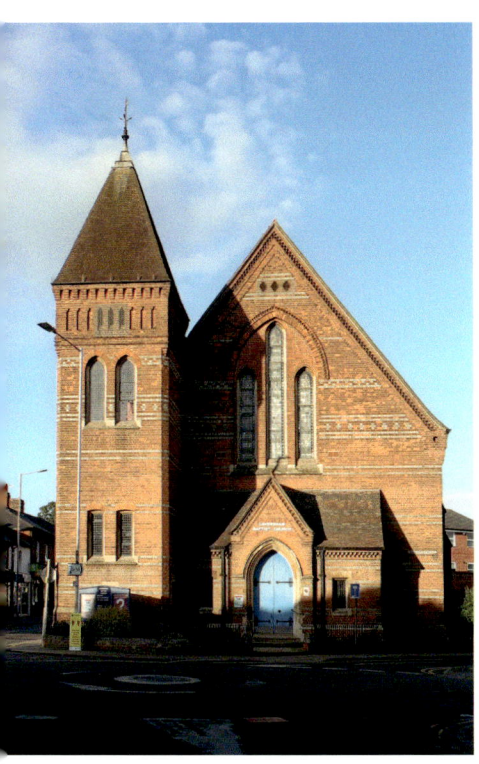

Caversham Baptist Church, Prospect Street

Opposite page:
Moulded brick and terracotta decorations grace walls and doorways, Elgar Road

1877: Yattendon Court, north-east of Newbury, for himself; long and asymmetrical with a four-storey tower; demolished. One wonders why, in 1926, its new owner knocked down what must have been a sound building. The same fate befell the architect's enormous Eaton Hall in Cheshire, which Pevsner ranked alongside other great mid-career works such as Manchester Town Hall, saying that Eaton 'seems to have been about as homely'.

1877–80: St Bartholomew's church, St Bartholomew's Road. Waterhouse did only the nave; the chancel, designed by G.F. Bodley and Thomas Garner, was not built until 1897.

1880–82: East Thorpe, Redlands Road, now the Museum of English Rural Life. The 20th-century extension, though in keeping, exacerbates a certain institutional look about Waterhouse's work.

1884–5: Buckhold, between Bradfield and Upper Basildon, now St Andrew's School; a large red-brick mansion with stone dressings; prominent corner turret. Pevsner says, 'large and quite freely grouped. Red brick and yellow terracotta. Gothic and Elizabethan forms mixed. Became a school 1935.'

H.S. Goodhart-Rendel, in *English Architecture since the Regency* (1953), says,

> Waterhouse is an architect whose stock at the moment is down at bottom… In matters of taste [posterity] is still coy when his work comes before it for judgement… Among the practitioners of this logical domestic Gothic, he surpassed all others in ability…'.

Having praised his 'large grasp of planning and mastery of architectural organisation', Goodhart-Rendel finds that 'In colour and texture… his buildings are usually so forbidding as to lead naturally to their being undervalued'. He compares St Paul's School, Hammersmith, to 'a piece of raw meat'.

Decorative brickwork in Reading and the region: the Victorian flowering

Jane A. Wight

Moulded brick and terracotta flowers – square panels or long courses of them – bloomed on grand and ordinary houses in Reading and other buildings in Victorian times. Thousands survive, perhaps a little obscured by grime and dust but intact. Even the smallest houses have these extravagant, significant details, which were made possible by plentiful, cheaply-paid labour. Relative prosperity, high employment and low wages were experienced at the same time. In the 1880s a small brick house might be built for as little as £80.

Fashions developed here in such a way that the cramped terrace house and the freestanding large house were built of the same material and ornamented similarly: the decoration varied in quantity or degree rather than in type. Brick is the dominant material, and the decorative work that was done in brick in the decades before the Kaiser's War (1916–1920) is unusually elaborate – a speciality of the area. The colouring is also local, with grey, purple or cream bricks complementing the main strong red. The flowers are always red.

This work is largely ignored or taken for granted; it is worth looking at, though. These Victorian and then Edwardian 'extras' were a constant (sometimes overdone) attempt to lessen the plainness of the spreading townscape. They were as respectable and fussy as the women's finest clothes. The close, square boxes of houses are done up, at the least, with ribbons of different coloured bricks.

Mini-battlements or fleur-de-lis or trefoils rampage along the peak of the roofs. Globes, conical spikes, heavy leaf curls or even fierce open-mouthed dragons rise above the gable ends. The distribution of dragons is limited though: one feels they were gauged rather risky or over-expensive

for the back streets. Even chimney stacks may be patterned, while chimney pots are daringly tall or ornamented with studs. There may be dentilated – sharp 'dog tooth' – courses of diagonally-laid bricks under the eaves, beside the coloured or moulded courses at the floor levels. And, finally overwhelming and irritating us with decoration, houses may carry panels of hung tiles – these with names and shapes like 'fish scale', 'fish tail', 'hammer head' and 'arrow head'.

All this brickwork was the product of an enormous boom in local brick-making demanded by a sharply-growing population – evidently with fancy ideas. Brick had been, for a long time, the main building material here. Despite the concrete office blocks it still is, but the majority of the bricks now come from Stewartby or Peterborough and other places on the deep 'Oxford clay' belt. This is a modern development that introduced the typical dull pinky-beige bricks which may be given a variety of dark or mottled facings by the manufacturers. The red is missing because the Oxford clay, unlike most of the shallower local clays, lacks the iron that causes bricks to fire 'brick red'.

The 'imported' bricks have conquered chiefly because they are cheaper. The main reasons for this are the size and purity of the Oxford clay deposits – making possible large-scale mechanization and production – and the fact that carbonaceous 'fossil fuel' in the clay keeps fuel costs low. These bricks practically fire themselves.

Special mouldings are fairly unusual in modern brickwork, whatever the source of the bricks. The really elaborate work was never revived after World War I. This applies not just to the flowers and mixed colours, but to details like door jambs and window surrounds with complex mouldings that imitated 15th- and 16th-century brickwork.

What is surprising, perhaps, is that Oxfordshire, Berkshire and the South generally played only a smallish part in the early development of brick. The medieval brick mouldings and ornament that provided some of the inspiration for the Victorian flowering belonged more especially to East Anglia and Essex. They were followed by long ages of plain or

Hung tiles (fishtail),
Liverpool Road

Ornamented chimneys

Opposite page:
Courses of yellow and 'dog tooth' brickwork dress this terraced house in Cumberland Road

Dangerous-looking finial, Elmhurst Road

simple brickwork, but also by the gradual and successful progress of the material in south-east England. Stone was still used where there were quarries, though even in the Middle Ages it was carried long distances for the greatest building works. Brick was well-established in Reading when, in the early 19th century, the Kennet & Avon canal broke the pattern by bringing in Bath limestone. This was also taken to Oxford, which was an old stone town built with limestone from Headington and the Cotswold quarries.

The Rev John Keble's foundation of Keble College at Oxford proved to be a real and shattering attack on the building traditions of Oxford. It was designed by the Gothic-Revivalist architect William Butterfield and took its first students in 1870. It has every kind of red brick moulding and fierce stripes of purplish-black brick, looking hectic and overdone among the weather-worn stones of Oxford. Out along the Banbury Road and the Woodstock Road though, North Oxford was now built up as a response to the domestic needs of the dons, who university regulations now allowed to marry. North Oxford is full of big houses for which multi-colours and

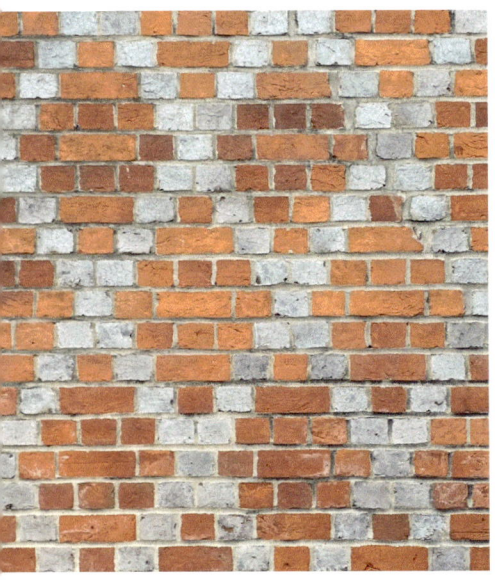

multi-mouldings of brick, as well as machine-cut limestone, were used. It lacks the harmony of variations on a theme that was sometimes achieved in Reading from the 1860s onward. Nor did the smaller brick houses share in the decoration to the same flamboyant extent as in Reading.

Brick had stayed plain from the Elizabethan age to the 18th century. Then some restrained swags of fruit and foliage were introduced, employed by Christopher Wren and many others. There were introduced the beautiful soft and rich red bricks that were set over windows and carriage archways – the close-set *voussoir* bricks. For the prosperous, dignified houses of brick decorated in these gentle ways were erected in London, Essex, the Home Counties, Berkshire, Hampshire and Sussex. Wiltshire kept mainly to the local limestones. The swags, or half garlands, would provide some inspiration for the Victorians. So did the practice of dipping unfired bricks in special grey-firing sand and using the grey faces for a wide or close chequerwork in the fabric of red brick houses, or for big panels of grey. These bricks gained a shallow, uneven glaze during firing from the sand. The technique continued in use throughout the Victorian and Edwardian periods, the grey bricks being used for courses, panels and diamond patterning. The purple or purplish-grey bricks were a Victorian invention, made by cutting down the oxygen reaching the kilns: these bricks have a hard, metallic appearance somehow reminiscent of coke and – I think – are never attractive. The widespread use of cream and yellowish bricks, made of chalky, iron-free clay, can also be oppressive.

The medieval and Tudor mouldings that were copied first by the Victorians survived in East Anglia, notably at East Barsham Manor House in Norfolk. They were popularized by such books as Augustus Welby Northmore Pugin's *Details of ancient houses of the 15th and 16th centuries,* which was published in 1836. A.W.N. Pugin was a dynamic and influential Gothic Revivalist who designed every kind of furniture as well as buildings. He died in 1852, aged only 40. The church of St James, beside the Forbury and the abbey ruins in Reading, is his work: it is, untypically for him, in the Norman style and built of flint and stone.

Moulded terracotta decoration, a fancy chimney, pierced ridge tiles, finials, even a dragon – the old Hillingdon Prince has it all

Opposite page:
Voussoir arch with red and grey chequerwork, Town Hall

Diamond pattern, Foxhill House

The brickmakers did not remain content with reviving late medieval or Tudor motifs. They soon pillaged the Renaissance also, with its formal acanthus foliage and flutings and renewed classical ornament. They took up Jacobean strapwork and monsters' and cherubs' faces, moulding these in terracotta, which is pure, dense brick – another Victorian rediscovery. They added ideas of their own, such as the panels of plump flowers and leaves, the fretted or pierced ridge tiles and some of the finials. Many workers, mechanization and efficient coal-firing allowed the brickmakers and tilers to produce, in thousands, ornaments that would once have been limited to rich properties – whether these ornaments were made in stone, brick or wood.

It should be noted that in the 18th century red brick had been condemned as vulgar or overassertive by some fashionable thinkers. This accounts for the building of houses with freestone or grey brick fronts to the street and red brick sides and back.

Vachel Almshouses, Castle Street

For the same reason, brick-built Regency houses were stuccoed over. Otherwise unpretentious houses in the earlier part of the 19th century were stuccoed and plastered and sometimes scored with lines to imitate stone masonry, as found in some houses on Castle Hill, Reading. Thus the mid and High Victorian choice of red brick – a return to the usual Tudor colouring – was itself a reaction. This is seen in Victorian Gothic or mock-Tudor almshouses in Reading.

The almshouse is one type of building that always attracted conservative or revivalist designers. Even in the mid-15th century, when a rebuilt parish church and a college, grammar school and almshouse were erected at Higham Ferrers in Northamptonshire, the almshouse was notably conservative and demure, while the other buildings were given the most up-to-date carved and fretted stonework. Old styles of building

Red sandstone and terracotta decoration, Town Hall

have been considered most suitable and reassuring for old people. This applies, for example, to St Bartholomew's Hospital at Newbury – founded in 1698 but built in what was then old-fashioned half-timbering – and to the almshouses in the churchyard of St Helen's at Abingdon.

The hamlet of Horncastle has long been absorbed into west Reading; its almshouses in New Lane Hill, erected in 1856, are typical of the Victorian return to Tudor style. A low rectangular building with added dormer windows, its decoration includes a diamond diaper of purplish bricks, and the pairs of chimneys are elegant imitations of the past, being tall and octagonal (p. 3).

In the centre of Reading, the rebuilding of the almshouses in Castle Street demonstrated both new fashions and new ambitions. The old stone panel (rediscovered in 1954 and re-set in an end wall) records the foundation of the 'Alms-Houses' in 1634 by Sir Thomas Vachel, who provided 'for the maintenance of six poor men' only. In 1866 the old building was sold for £510; that, and £4232.16s 5d collected through an appeal, was used to provide for 24 people, who were given an enclave of buildings, like a narrow street, to live in (see 'A walking tour'). At the Castle Street end are small square towers, straight out of the Tudor age. The walls have purple-grey diapering. Along the rooflines though, bowl fine 'modern' ridge tiles, with three wide circles to a tile.

Even more fancy 'Tudor' brick was sometimes used. A good example of this is no. 9 Tilehurst Road, built as a private house in 1854. This has diapering and all sorts of moulded brick and is crowned by octagonal chimneys with spiked 'star tops'.

The later and more ambitious institutional buildings, and even shops, were given more detailed brick or terracotta ornament taken from different ages and places. The southern end of Reading Town Hall, designed by Alfred Waterhouse (1875) was built of grey and red brick, evidently on a Dutch model. The remaining parts, by Thomas Lainson (1882) and W.R. Howell (1897), use darker greys and some red sandstone. The mixtures make for heaviness. Queen Victoria Street is a High Victorian

Opposite page:
WI Palmer Memorial Hall, West Street

development, its buildings all exactly alike and loaded with deep red terracotta ornament (see 'A walking tour'). An imitative adjoining building in Broad Street carries the date 1894. Renaissance motifs were used for this work. Cream terracotta decorations, freer and rather gentler, were used for buildings in Station Road and for the West Street Hall or W.I. Palmer Memorial Hall (see 'A walking tour').

One of the nicest buildings stood in Blagrave Street. It had late Victorian moulded brick, detailed but not heavy. The mouldings were classical 'egg and dart' (ovals alternating with arrow heads). There were fine panels of long-whiskered barley and a triangular panel of agricultural implements and corn stooks. Over all were 'sculptures' of the lion and the unicorn supporting the Royal Arms. Beautiful work, alas it was coated with white paint and has since been demolished.

In a very different style, but because they are also exceptionally fine work, I note here the two magnificent dragon finials on the former Imperial Hotel (1897) opposite Henley station. The smaller has the traditional arched and fire-spitting posture, with creased neck and very flyaway wings. The larger, about three feet tall, stands upright like the supporter of a heraldic shield. It has big circular scales to its chest and separate great features to its wings.

Reading shared many kinds of clay product with other areas, both Victorian and pre-Victorian. Tile-hanging, for instance, was favoured in Sussex and Hampshire long before the tiles could be stamped out by machinery. The Fareham (Hampshire) speciality of chimney pots – known as 'reds' and 'long Farehams' – was like Reading's choice of red pots or 'tallboys'. Some tallboys are seven and a half feet high; three-footers are common. One great 19th-century change was the use of the cheap grey Welsh slates for roofs: production of the traditional ceramic tiles then shrank away. The slates, though, were used in combination with curved or V-shaped ridge tiles – and the elaboration of these was a part of the Reading extravaganza. No Reading work though, can rival in eccentric complexity 'Massey's Folly' (1870–1919), the brick building later used as

the village school in Farringdon, Hampshire. This should be studied, but not taken as typical of anything at all.

There were dozens of brickmaking and tiling firms, especially around Reading and Bracknell. The outstanding producers were S & E Collier, 'Tilemakers and Brickmakers', a firm which lasted from 1853 or earlier to 1967, with works at Elgar Road, Water Road and Coley Avenue. In 1908 they bought out their rivals Poulton and Son. Colliers' bricks and roof furniture created whole streets of West Reading; houses, but also churches (St Saviour's) and schools (Katesgrove – see 'A walking tour'). Elgar Road itself was named and being built by 1884. The house on the corner of Waterloo Road carries a showcase of decorative work on its south side and was evidently attached to the works. The houses all have slate roofs, but that is their only plainness. They even have flowered or fluted 'keystones', complex courses of classical 'guioche' (circular twists) and mouldings that imitate rope, with minute anchors at their ends. A row of three small cottages in River Road relies on different colours, not mouldings, for ornament. They have the very common stripes of cream brick and overweight zigzags down the corners (quoins). There are also two unusual details: a countersunk, stepped cross of purple bricks on one gable-end, and a large, ingenious roundel of red and cream bricks on the other; both precise and inventive work (see 'A walking tour').

Only two companies survived into the 1990s: Whitehall Brick and Tile Works at Arborfield and the Star Works at Knowl Hill. Closures were not just the result of economic forces; in some cases the clay deposits had simply been worked out. One ghost of the industry remains in Reading: a new development off Honey End Lane is named Chimney Court, where Colliers' large square chimney used to stand.

Brick is very strong; the local product remains in the streets, especially those small houses whose prices have skyrocketed. A walk down Cholmeley Road in Newtown is revelatory, if we use our eyes. Paint, cement or roughcast has hidden some of the work; some has been suddenly made vivid with Caribbean or Bangladeshi colours.

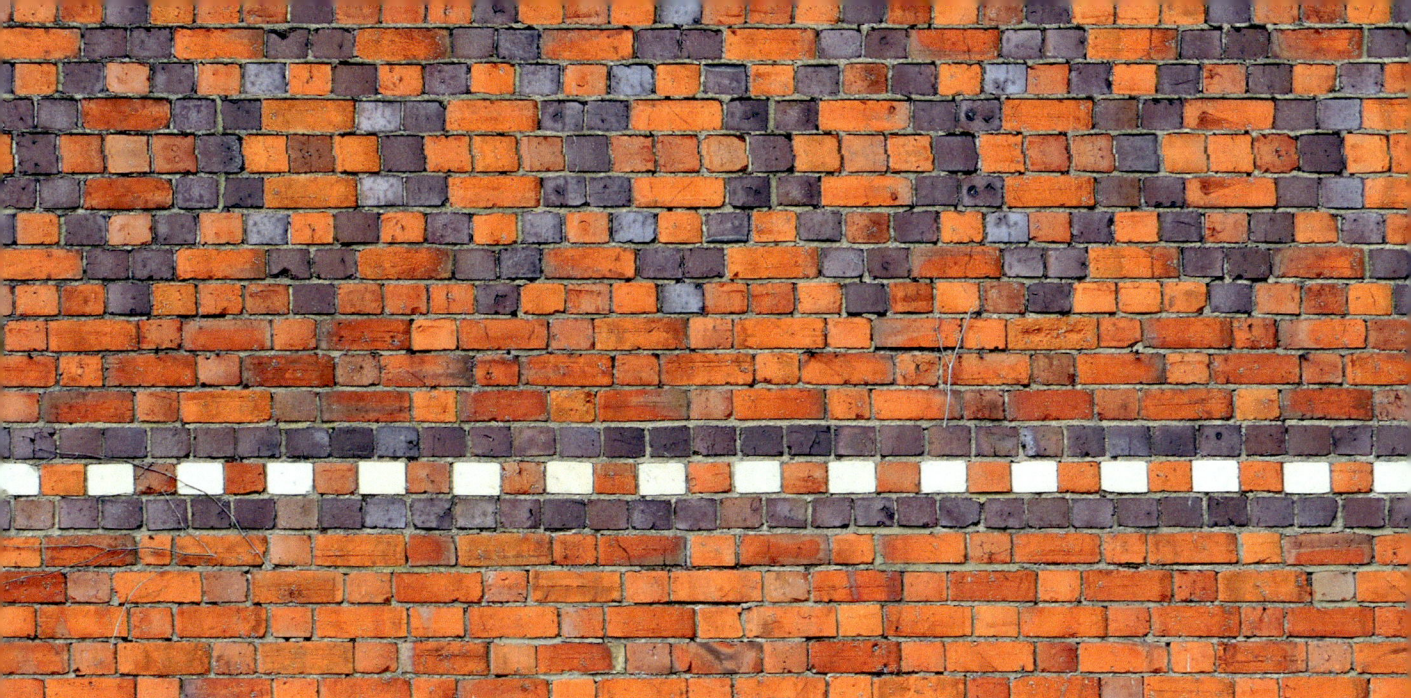

Multi-coloured brickwork at River Road

Opposite page:
Stepped cross of purple bricks, River Road

Roundel of red and cream bricks, River Road

Love your brickwork: Preserve and conserve

Over the 20th century Parliament has passed various pieces of legislation intended to preserve the better bits of our built environment from destruction or spoiling. The most demolition-proof is the Schedule of Monuments; formerly known as Ancient Monuments, they can be as young as the 1788 High Bridge (Duke Street) across the Kennet. Far more numerous are Listed Buildings and Structures, which originally came in three grades, denoting national, regional or local importance. Grade III was abolished in 1970: many of them had been spoilt and no longer qualified, but many others became part of Conservation Areas. Later, a new intermediate Grade II* was introduced. Some Planning Authorities instituted Local Lists, which have no legal force but do warn developers that they may face a bit of a fight. No listing grade is an absolute guarantee of preservation. Then there are Conservation Areas, which may or may not

Junction Road

Field Road diamond

Opposite page:
Wokingham Road

School Terrace

contain listed buildings. Between them, Reading's 15 Conservation Areas and hundreds of Grade II listings cover much of our Georgian and Victorian heritage. Finally, and least-known, are Article 4 Directives: stronger than Conservation Areas, they remove certain development rights. Reading has chosen to apply this measure mainly to streets and parts of streets that display some of the best brick patterns and polychromy. They are:

- Basingstoke Road (St Leonard's Terrace), 2–16 even:
  Grey patterned brickwork
- Brisbane Road, 3–27 odd: Grey patterned brickwork
- Field Road, 3–49 odd: Patterned brickwork (see 'A walking tour')
- Jesse Terrace, 1–35: Patterned brickwork
- Junction Road, 23–31 odd: Grey patterned brickwork
- Katesgrove Lane, 84–92 even: Patterned brickwork
- Polstead Road, 1–33 odd: Patterned brickwork
- Prince of Wales Avenue, 48–54 even: Patterned brickwork
- Rectory Road, 8–32 even, 1–17 odd: Patterned brickwork

- River Road, Katesgrove, 1–7: Patterned brickwork (see 'A walking tour')
- School Terrace, 1–31: Decorative brickwork
- Shaftesbury Road, 73–103 odd: Patterned brickwork and terracotta details
- Wantage Road, 4–34 even: Patterned brickwork
- Wokingham Road, 1–19 odd: Grey patterned brickwork

Unfortunately, the Council lacks the resources to properly monitor all these locations and enforce the regulations; but in 1985 they did try to raise people's awareness of conservation matters by putting out a leaflet full of good advice for owners of old houses. As well as the treatment or mistreatment of brickwork, it covered doors, windows, guttering etc. The leaflet has some excellent line drawings; alas the only colour featured is a nasty and un-Reading mustardy yellow.

Reading Abbey's Hospitium of St John still stands to the north of St Laurence's graveyard

Opposite page:
Reading Town Hall

III. A walking tour:
Town centre & Katesgrove

This tour starts in Town Hall Square. From here you can see a great deal of brickwork: some real Georgian, a lot of neo-Georgian of various dates and varying degrees of convincingness, much Victoriana, and several examples of modern, non-load-bearing brick cladding on steel-framed blocks; there are even bricks under your feet.

Hospitium of St John the Baptist
But before you examine the municipal buildings, turn down the alley between Blandy & Blandy's and St Laurence's church, take a left and walk towards and around the end of the Reading Abbey's Hospitium (now the Co-op day nursery). This late 15th-century building is made mostly of flint and rubble, but the stair turret on the north side is probably Reading's oldest brickwork. The bond is trying to be English; irregularities stem from the somewhat random, non-standardised brick sizes.

Town Hall

Retrace your steps, noting en route the only exterior view of the Flemish bond town hall of 1785, a plain Georgian box now misleadingly called the Victoria Hall.

The rest of the Town Hall complex came in three phases, starting with Waterhouse's light grey end of 1872 with the clocktower. By 1882 the Council wanted an extension with a large hall; Waterhouse was too busy or too expensive, so they staged a competition. The judge was Thomas Lainson, a Brighton man who happened to be architect to the estates of Reading's MP. Three prizes were awarded, but none of the winners got the job: it went to Lainson himself, causing quite a stir. The Art Gallery extension by Cooper and Howells (1897) merely followed Lainson's design (look out for the air bricks mentioned on p. 32). Starting just around the corner in Valpy Street, unfinished friezes in terracotta and sandstone high up depict ancient Britons, philosophers, poets etc., coming up-to-date

Ordinary bricks laid at odd angles make up a frieze at Chancellors, Market Place

Cut brickwork on the upper storeys of Market House

Opposite page:
Victoria Hall, Town Hall

Different coloured greys due to phased extension

An unfinished frieze in terracotta and sandstone – blank panels either side

with Edison and his telephone and Maxim with his gun. Local sculptor W. Charles May worked the figures, which were cast by S & E Collier. When Architects Design Partnership restored the building in 1989, they had to order 69 different 'special' bricks in non-standard shapes and sizes to go round corners and make up arches.

Market Place
Proceed to the top end of the triangular Market Place. Keep right to Buttermarket; ahead, the top of Chancellors on the corner has a decorative frieze made largely with ordinary bricks laid at odd angles. At the third corner, across the High Street, Market House has a fine display of cut brickwork on the upper storeys.

Curved bricks at Abbey Corner

Dukesbridge House:
a change of name would be tricky

Opposite page:
The former Central Club

An example of 'tuck pointing'

Victorian brick patterning at 47 London Street

Duke Street

Proceed down High Street to the crossroads. Abbey Corner on the Kings Road/Duke Street corner has very slightly curved bricks.

Cross into Duke Street and just before the High Bridge, look up to the left: the name 'Dukesbridge House' is cut into the wall set back behind the roadside buildings; a change of name would be tricky. (The south flank of John Lewis on Minster Street still bears the name 'Heelas' similarly carved.) Cross the road and walk back to turn left into Thorn Lane and through to Yield Hall Place and the bridge over the Kennet. Look ahead at the prefabricated curved panels on Debenhams: no individual bricks were laid here. As you pass the London Street Brasserie on the left, note the tightly-curved section calling for Header bond. On the right, the windows in the eastern end of the Oracle Riverside have impossibly long, flat arches that cannot be self-supporting.

London Street

Cross over to the Casino, then cross the A329 to see, on your left, the Great Expectations pub, built in 1843 as a Mechanics' Institute. Guidebooks call this a Bath stone building, but the side and rear walls are brick.

The former Central Club on the corner opposite started life as a garage for police cars. Its architect or builder took some care to avoid the monotony of a plain brick wall all on one plane.

Up the street, nos. 47 and 49 flank an alleyway: the left-hand wall boasts a large and beautifully laid display of Victorian patterning. Its close proximity to a house that was there in 1518 shows how deeply ingrained the patterning habit had become; the builder was not bothered that very few people would notice or admire his work. Further on, no. 101 has a small example of slate-hanging on the right gable, visible only once you have crossed the street.

Back down at no. 86 is a specimen of 'tuck pointing'. A Georgian ideal was to make the joints between bricks as fine as possible; if you lacked the skill to do so, you could cheat by colouring the mortar to match the bricks, gouging a narrow groove and filling it with fine white putty. Unfortunately, it is hard to match the mortar to the bricks in colour or texture, and sooner or later the putty falls out; nobody is fooled.

Header bond, Church Street

A stretch of Flemish Garden Wall, Church Street

Opposite page:
River Road cottages

Katesgrove Primary School

AD 1888 set in bricks on a gable, Garnet Street

Church Street

Half way up the hill, turn west into Church Street for no. 11: by no means a large or prestigious house, but it uses the expensive Header bond. At the far end, opposite St Giles-in-Reading, is a stretch of Flemish Garden Wall.

Pell Street and Elgar Road

Turn left up Southampton Street and right into Pell Street. The Gables on the left have made an effort with a kind of neo-Reading style.

Follow Pell Street to the Katesgrove Lane/Elgar Road junction. You are now entering the heartland of Reading fancy brickwork: examples from around here are illustrated in 'bricky' literature.

The corner shop used to be the Kennet Arms; from its garden you could see the end of a notable crinkle-crankle wall. Elgar Road itself used to be known as a sort of outdoor catalogue displaying the wares of the several brickworks in the area, especially panels, swags and keystones (it is still worth a stroll although many of the houses have been spoilt in the usual ways).

Katesgrove Lane and River Road

Cross over into Katesgrove Lane and turn left into River Road to admire the famous roundel (see p. 48) and much else. When you re-emerge on to Katesgrove Lane, note also Katesgrove Primary School across the road.

Berkeley Avenue and Garnet Street

Return to the crossroads and turn right into Berkeley Avenue; as you cross the canal, look back to see the design on the gable of the last house on River Road. Carry on over the main road and Holy Brook, then slope down into St Paul's Court on your right. Take one of the footpaths on your right to make your way along the bank of the Brook to Brook Street West.

Turn into Garnet Street; notice the date AD 1888 in bricks.

Rat-trap bond painted black

Carey Baptist Church: a change from the mainly red Anglican churches of the period

Opposite page:
Glazed-brick frontage, Castle Tap

Window arches across differently shaped convex bays, Castle Street

The former Cross Keys pub

Garnet Street and Field Road

Cross Wolseley Street; there is a house on the right in Chinese or Rat-trap bond, alas painted black. The garden wall beyond used to show the bond more clearly but has since been rendered. Cross Dover Street, then turn right into Field Road (where the subterranean chalk mines caused the partial collapse of two houses in 2000) and then left up Castle Hill/Bath Road. Cross over at the traffic lights and continue just past Lima Court. Between it and the Spire Dunedin Hospital is a crinkle-crankle: short and low, but the one in town that you can see properly.

Russell Street, Baker Street and Carey Street

Cross Russell Street and follow it down, bearing right, until you reach the crossroads with Baker Street. Note the Presbytery on the opposite corner. Turn right onto Baker Street, then right on to Carey Street and walk up to Carey Baptist Church of 1870, described by Pevsner as 'high-shouldered and masculine'. The west front is a colourful composition with some tumbling-in and some Italian-looking gothic arches – a change from the mainly red Anglican churches of the period.

Castle Hill and Castle Street

Turn left on to Castle Hill again where the Castle Tap, like many pubs, has a glazed-brick frontage, perhaps to facilitate cleaning up after a messy Saturday night.

Cross the roundabout into Castle Street, which shows plenty of brickwork on both sides. On the right are the Almshouses, followed by a well-kept and unspoilt Georgian sequence; better indeed than London Street. No. 39 is clearly a pastiche, but forgivable in the setting. The architect was persuaded to use Flemish bond, and the not-quite-Reading colour is gently saying 'Yes, it's a copy'.

On the other side of the street, the Courts and Police Station perhaps pandered to those who say 'I don't mind what you build in Reading as long as it's brick': deadly dull red stretchers. Past the Courts, the Sun Inn is partly tile-hung.

At the bottom of Castle Street on the right, nos. 3–5 have window arches across two differently shaped convex bays: 2D curves that would have required extremely accurate cutting of each brick. In 1877, the Cross Keys, which Pevsner rates Reading's best Victorian pub, stood on the south east corner of the cross roads – and still does, complete with tile-hanging.

Hosier Street and Düsseldorf Way

Turn left into St Mary's Butts, then left into Hosier Street and on to Düsseldorf Way to admire the Burglar bond on the flank of the Broad Street Mall. Return to the half-timbered building on the corner of Hosier Street for a fine display of brick nogging, with bricks arranged in patterns inside wooden frames.

Further along on the right, the large modern building on the corner of Broad Street has what might be called frame-less nogging in a nice basket-weave.

Broad Street and West Street

Look to the left into Broad Street: the former McIlroys store on the opposite side is a fantastical pile with much glazed brickwork, and the proprietor's name appears in huge letters below the gable.

On into West Street, where the W.I. Palmer Memorial Building at nos. 41–43 shows a wealth of terracotta detail (see p. 46).

Friar Street

Turn right and walk down Friar Street; at nos. 29–31, Ajilon House, the former Atheneum Club, has a chunky terracotta front with flat arches using keys or notches to keep them up.

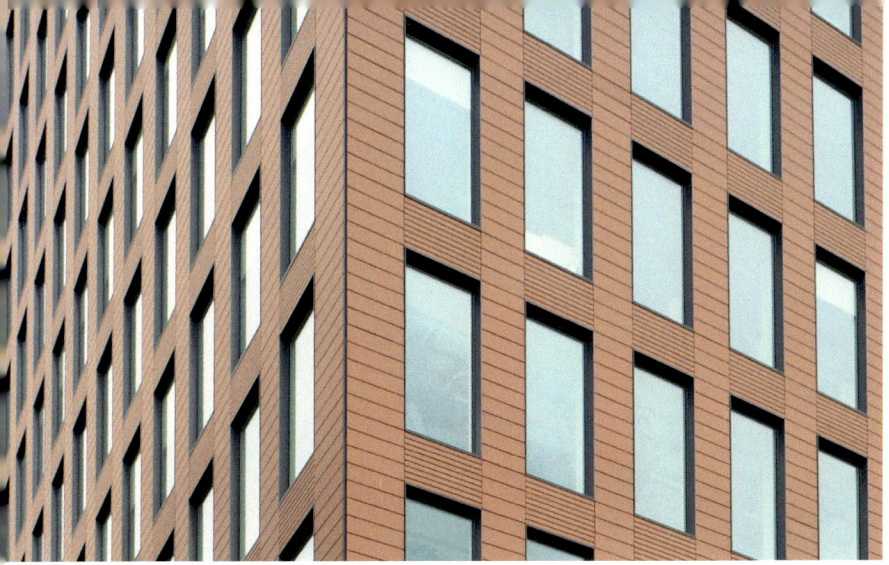 

The terracotta-clad Thames Tower opposite Reading Station

A pedestrian subway lined with blue and white brick/tiles that evoke the waves of the River Thames as you approach

Opposite page:
Bricks are arranged in patterns inside wooden frames on this half-timbered building in Hosier Street

Ajilon House, Friar Street

McIlroy Building, Oxford Road

Queen Victoria Street and Station Road

Queen Victoria Street, further along on the right, is a splendid red canyon that glows wonderfully in late, low winter sunshine. Turn into Station Road opposite; on the left, it has the remains of an exuberant terracotta range, of which the two middle portions fell down. One has been replaced with plain brick, matching the colours but not the forms of the original; the other is a simple grey, glassy affair.

So to the 1867 portion of the railway station, now the Three Guineas, which for some reason shunned the local materials and brought in white bricks from Shropshire.

Finally, having started this tour in the late 15th century, we end with two very recent examples: the Thames Tower opposite the station, re-clad in 2016 with real terracotta at the insistence of Reading Borough Council; and the pedestrian subway under the station, opened in 2013, that takes you towards the Thames towpath and is lined with an evolving pattern of blue and white bricks/tiles that gradually turns a deeper blue as you approach the river.

Two Rivers Press has been publishing in and about Reading since 1994. Founded by the artist Peter Hay (1951–2003), the press continues to delight readers, local and further afield, with its varied list of individually designed, thought-provoking books.